CELEBRATE HARLEM!

by Daphne Greaves

Harcourt
SCHOOL PUBLISHERS

Cover, ©Erik Freeland/Corbis; p.3, ©AP Photo/Jim Cooper; p.4, ©AP Photo/Matt Moyer; p.5, ©Bettmann/CORBIS; p.6, ©AP Photo/Diane Bondareff; p.7, ©Keith Bedford/Getty Images; p.8, Chester Higgins, Jr.; p.9, ©Lee Snider/Photo Images/CORBIS; p.10, ©Leo Rosenthal/Pix Inc./Time Life Pictures/Getty Images; p.11, p.12, ©Bettmann/CORBIS; p.13, ©Chris Hondros/Getty Images; p.14, ©Robert A. Sabo/Getty Images.

Printed in China

ISBN 10: 0-15-351540-6
ISBN 13: 978-0-15-351540-8

Ordering Options
ISBN 10: 0-15-351214-8 (Grade 4 Advanced Collection)
ISBN 13: 978-0-15-351214-8 (Grade 4 Advanced Collection)
ISBN 10: 0-15-358130-1 (package of 5)
ISBN 13: 978-0-15-358130-4 (package of 5)

5 6 7 8 9 10 985 12 11 10 09

Characters

Announcer	Mr. Boyd	Maria
Akello	Lisha	John
Tasha	Mr. Bascomb	Melissa
Ms. Hanson	Professor Rivera	

Setting: Various locations in Harlem, a neighborhood in New York City

Announcer: From the television studios of Madame C.J. Walker Elementary School, Mr. Swan's fourth-grade class proudly presents *Celebrate Harlem!* with your hosts Akello Cash and Maria Lopez.

Akello: Welcome. When Mr. Swan began a unit on Harlem, we were knocked out by the awesome aspects of its history.

Maria: It's made us even more proud of our community. We huddled together and decided we wanted to share what we learned, so we created this special program.

Akello: Get ready to learn about a remarkable New York City neighborhood as we journey to some famous Harlem destinations.

Akello: You know, Maria, there's so much to learn about Harlem that I'm not quite sure where to start.

Maria: Just remember what Mr. Swan always says. When you want to learn something—

Maria and Akello: A good place to start is the library!

Akello: Harlem has a very special library.

Maria: Student reporter Tasha Johnson has the story.

Tasha: Thanks, Akello and Maria. I'm here with librarian George Bascomb. Can you tell us a bit about the library?

Mr. Bascomb: The Schomburg Center for Research in Black Culture is a national research library. Our goal is to reconstruct the experiences of people of African descent throughout the world.

Arturo Alfonso Schomburg

Tasha: How did the library get its name?

Mr. Bascomb: It's named for Arturo Alfonso Schomburg.
He was an African American scholar who was born in 1874.
Throughout his life, Schomburg had a thirst to learn as much
as he could about the history of people of African descent.

Tasha: Did he ever come to America?

Mr. Bascomb: Oh, yes! As I recall, he lived in New York from
1891, until his death in 1938. Many of the books he owned are
now part of the library's collection.

Tasha: I guess we owe him a lot.

Mr. Bascomb: We certainly do, Tasha. I encourage you and
anyone else who wants to learn about Harlem to visit our library.

Tasha: Thanks, Mr. Bascomb, that's a great idea. I'll be
spending a lot of time here. That's all for now, Akello and Maria.

Maria: Thanks, Tasha. Tell me, Akello, if you had only one day to show visitors Harlem, where would you take them?

Akello: Well, definitely the Apollo Theatre, Hamilton Heights, the Studio Museum, the Boys Choir of Harlem, Strivers' Row, the Dance Theatre of Harlem, Sugar Hill, Hamilton Heights—

Maria: Hold on, Akello, I said a day not a week!

Akello: Harlem may only extend from 110th Street to 155th Street, but there's just so much to see!

Maria: Unfortunately, we don't have time to see everything, but our student reporters will select some of the highlights for us.

Akello: Lisha Haynes starts us off.

Lisha: I'm at the Studio Museum in Harlem. Taylor Boyd is a guide here, and he intends to tell us all about the museum.

Mr. Boyd: The Studio Museum in Harlem opened in 1967. Our art consists of works by African American artists, as well as Caribbean and African artists. We also have a collection of traditional African art.

Lisha: Sounds like there's a lot to see. Do you have a favorite artist?

Mr. Boyd: I love them all! However, one of my favorites is an artist raised right here in Harlem. His name was Romare Bearden, and he was one of the founders of this museum. After serving in the military in World War II, he came back to New York and had exhibitions of his work.

Lisha: What is his art like?

Mr. Boyd: Romare Bearden was most famous for his collages.

Lisha: Collage art is made by pasting colored paper, cloth, and even objects like bottle caps or buttons on paper to make a picture.

Mr. Boyd: That's right, some collages are very ornate. Much of Romare Bearden's art was inspired by what he saw around him in Harlem. For example, his collage called *The Dove* shows a vigorous and festive Harlem street scene.

Lisha: Thanks for talking with us, Mr. Boyd. Anyone who would like the opportunity to see some wonderful art should visit the Studio Museum in Harlem. Back to you, Maria and Akello.

Romare Bearden

Maria: Thanks, Lisha.

Akello: Now let's go to student reporter John Brown.

John: No trip to Harlem is complete without a visit to the area known as Strivers' Row. I'm speaking here with Professor Elizabeth Rivera, an expert on the area. Welcome to the program, Professor Rivera.

Prof. Rivera: What a gorgeous day for a walk on Strivers' Row.

John: Where exactly are we?

Prof. Rivera: Strivers' Row runs along 138th and 139th Streets in Harlem. The beautiful brownstone houses on these streets were built in the 1890s.

Member of Congress Adam Clayton Powell, Jr.

John: Look at the gates on the alleyways. This one has an old sign that says, "Walk Your Horses."

Prof. Rivera: That's right. The houses all have courtyards in the back. At one time, these alleys were used by delivery people on horses who brought supplies around to the back of the houses.

John: How did the area get the name Strivers' Row?

Prof. Rivera: Around the 1920s, many African Americans who were wealthy began moving into the area. They were ambitious, and people referred to them as *strivers*, so these blocks they lived on became known as *Strivers' Row*.

John: Who were they?

Prof. Rivera: The residents included doctors and lawyers. African American architect Vertner Tandy lived here. So did the musician Eubie Blake, heavyweight boxer Harry Wills, and Congressman Adam Clayton Powell, Jr., to name just a few.

John: Thanks for your time, Professor Rivera. I'd say Strivers' Row is definitely worth a visit. Back to you, Akello and Maria.

Akello: Thanks for that terrific story, John.

Maria: Let's go right to student reporter Melissa Tate with a story about another Harlem striver.

Melissa: I'm standing in front of the Countee Cullen Branch Library on 136th Street in Harlem. Next to me is historian Malika Hanson. Ms. Hanson, why are we here?

Ms. Hanson: Well, Melissa, at one time this was the site of a townhouse owned by the first self-made African American woman millionaire. Her name was Madam C.J. Walker.

Melissa: Wait a minute. I recognize that name! Are you talking about the person our elementary school is named after?

Ms. Hanson: The very one.

Melissa: What can you tell us about her?

Madam C.J. Walker

Ms. Hanson: Madam Walker was born in 1867. She worked her way up from being a farm worker and doing laundry for others to owning her own business.

Melissa: How did she go into business?

Ms. Hanson: Well, it happened because of a bit of misfortune. When Madam Walker was in her twenties, her hair began to fall out, so she began experimenting with homemade hair products. After using each product, she expectantly examined her hair. She finally discovered a suitable product that made her hair grow back. She went into business selling this hair product. Within fifteen years, she had made a fortune.

Melissa: So then she built herself a beautiful house?

Ms. Hanson: Yes, she enjoyed her success, but she also gave back to the community. She donated large sums of money to the National Association for the Advancement of Colored People (NAACP). She also supported African American schools, orphanages, retirement homes, and the YWCA and YMCA.

Melissa: Now that's what I call a true success story. Back to you, Akello and Maria.

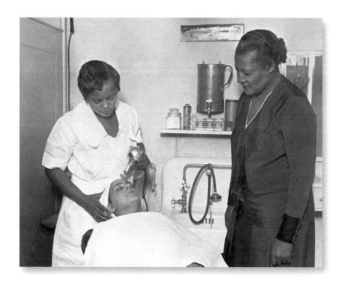

Akello: It just goes to show you that Harlem has always been a community of ambitious and successful people.

Maria: Absolutely, and one of Harlem's newer residents fits right in. In 2001, former President Bill Clinton opened an office on 125th Street in Harlem.

Akello: The President said he chose Harlem because he believes Harlem is a place where people hold up their heads and care about their neighbors.

Maria: President Clinton also said Harlem is a place filled with the rhythm of life and a song in its heart.

Akello: Wow, Maria, what a great lead-in to our last segment! We go now to the world famous Apollo Theatre.

Maria: There's no better place to symbolize the song in Harlem's heart.

Akello: Ever since 1934, stars such as Ella Fitzgerald, Bill Cosby, and Lauryn Hill have gotten their start at the Apollo's amateur night.

Maria: Today, from the Apollo, we'll hear our very own school chorus singing a famous song about our hometown, Harlem.

Announcer: Ladies and gentlemen, the Madame C.J. Walker Elementary School Chorus will now sing Billy Strayhorn's song, "Take the 'A' Train."

Chorus: You must take the "A" train
To go to Sugar Hill way up in Harlem . . .
Hurry, get on, now it's coming . . .
Soon you will be on Sugar Hill in Harlem.

Think Critically

1. What was the overall goal of Akello's and Maria's program, *Celebrate Harlem!*?

2. What details does the author give about the Studio Museum?

3. What did Mr. Swan tell his students was the best way to begin a research project?

4. What did the people who lived on Strivers' Row have in common?

5. What do you think the life of Madam C.J. Walker teaches us about success?

 **Social Studies**

Find Out About Your Town Be an investigator and find out about your hometown. What is the population? Who is the mayor? What county is your hometown in? Write a brief report on your findings.

School-Home Connection Take turns with friends or family members reading the various roles in this Readers' Theater. Remember to speak clearly and with the proper feeling!

Word Count: 1,483 (1,502)